T0364320

WHIMS *&* MOODS

WHIMS

AND

MOODS

BY

THOMAS THORNELY

CAMBRIDGE

At the University Press

1930

CAMBRIDGE
UNIVERSITY PRESS

University Printing House, Cambridge CB2 8BS, United Kingdom

Cambridge University Press is part of the University of Cambridge.

It furthers the University's mission by disseminating knowledge in the pursuit of education, learning and research at the highest international levels of excellence.

www.cambridge.org
Information on this title: www.cambridge.org/9781107486621

© Cambridge University Press 1930

First published 1930
First paperback edition 2015

A catalogue record for this publication is available from the British Library

ISBN 978-1-107-48662-1 Paperback

To

MY WIFE

ACKNOWLEDGEMENTS

I wish to thank the Editors of the Observer, *the* Spectator *and the* London Mercury *for their kindness in allowing me to include in this volume many pieces of verse which have appeared in their pages.*

T. THORNELY

MERTON HALL
CAMBRIDGE

Contents

Apologia Pro Libro Meo

WHEN old Menoetes floundered in the sea,
To the great joy of all his company,
No Teucrian louder laughed than some may
laugh at me,

In age-worn barge, long blistering on the shore
Of a smooth haven, putting forth once more,
With new-caulked seams, patched sail, and renovated
oar;

Venturing, verse-laden, into lyric seas
So thick with sails some scarce can catch a breeze;
'Whom does the interloping huckster think to
please?'

Some ask.—I answer, 'Should his bales beguile
One doldrum hour, provoking thought or smile,
Give the poor trader leave to think it worth his
while.'

Retirement

IF, on the top of his Tartarean hill,
  The torturing stone of Sisyphus were still;
  If the Tantalean wave should woo the lip;
Ixion's wheel rest like becalmèd ship;
Would the freed sufferers long that ease enjoy,
Or cast regretful glances on their late employ?

I know them all, for here they all repair,
To physic opulence with healing air.
Sir Tantalus is sinking to his grave,
Killed by the fond compliance of his wave;
Ixion, wiser, still can pleasure feel,
Lending his aid to turn another's wheel,
While Sisyphus (of Sisyphus and Co.)
Hopes soon to start his stone from its old place
  below.

Three Score & Ten

AGE is not all unkind: that ebbing tide,
  So sadly sung for what it bears away,
  Has drained the shallows where we launched
  our pride;
But sounder barks on surer seas abide,
Fraught with our hopes today.

Age is not all unkind: the shrinking wave
Has bared a reef, where with sea-wrack have lain,
While winds of noon's upraising round them rave,
Some gifts of grace life's innocent morning gave,
And evening finds again.

Age is not all unkind: the labouring wings,
For all their troublous beat, have stirred a sense,
That in the shadow of departing things,
As through life's droning griefs, there something
    sings
Of peace and recompense.

A Last Prayer

O WERE it mine to win unchallenged way
    (Presumptuous thought!) where Zion's
        braveries are,
Where saints, more bright than summer lightning's
    play,
Send their loud adorations pealing far
Through jewelled courts of day;
Still one last prayer it would be mine to pray—
Leave, sometimes leave, those gates of pearl ajar!

That I may steal from too ebullient bliss,
And on a less delirious beauty feed,
In some cool dell where lights and shadows kiss,
And (Take it not amiss,
Far-sounding Seraphs!) not a note is heard
Of harp or viol, only the piping reed
Of woodland rill and unbedizened bird.

Dreams & Freudians

THOU hast found slanderers, Sleep! who cast
    foul scorn
  On the bright-imaged forms that round thy
    throne
Flit nightly; proving them ignobly born,
  Things of vile import, symbolled or foreshown.

Fling back their scorn! though, in their impish way,
  Thy dream-sprites frolic with night's reverend
    hours,
The most are pure as children at their play,
  Or Carnival amazons with their battling flowers.

Their sage maligners, steeped in thoughts that spring
  From the sad haunts of maimed, afflicted mind,
To Dreamland's fountained courts and parterres
    bring
  The poisoned air of lazarets left behind.

By the veiled horror of such scenes obsessed,
  Imputing to the many what the few,
When the veil lifts, reveal, they know no rest,
  Till they prove vile Sleep's whole blithe innocent
    crew.

Dance on! in gay defiant disarray,
  Ye merry-hearted mummers of the night!
While your browed slanderers grope their peevish
    way,
  By one malodorous candle's treacherous light.

Pillage & Litter

Had I thy powers, O Pan!—
  Thy voice of thunder, thine avenging bees—
  The nameless fear should leap on many a man
In this fair tract of trees;
The pilfering horde should run, as once they ran
Who dared to desecrate thy sanctuaries.

Mark where their trail has gone—
Uprooted flowers, burnt heath, and litter spread—
As though some basilisk's eye had glared upon
Earth's beauty; Pan is dead,
Or that dread note men heard at Marathon
Had sounded here, as when the Persian fled.

Yet has he votaries still,
Who make his service their ennobling care;
Who hear his piping in each reed and rill
That moves in woodland air.
May these, O Pan! may these thy prophets fill
Impoverished hearts with love of all things fair.

Monkey Tricks

If some engrafted gland,
  Or bestial blood by daring hands injected
  From simian veins, with simian taints infected,
Could stay death's hand,
And yield us decades more of spurious being,
Beyond the meagre bounds of fate's decreeing,
Should we wave back the worms,
And take on grosser terms
The gift Tithonus rued, and Saturn's son rejected?

No! better it were to die
Even though that death were sleep that knows no
    waking,
Than by Medean arts win such re-making;
So, pass that folly by:
Let man and brute keep each his inborn organs;
We want no man-made monsters—fauns or gorgons;
Our blood's impure enough
Without imported stuff,
And bestial traits abound without this new-found
    faking.

Fenland in Winter

As like a dirge as ever blew
    The East-wind wailed along the fen;
    It drained each tussock of its dew,
And with a shroud of sickly hue
Wrapped home and byre of lonely men;
I fled, as from a basilisk's den.

But from the reeds there rose a cry,
(Or so it seemed) 'O come again
When summer blue is on the sky,
And up and down the dragon-fly,
A burnished knight with jewelled rein,
Pricks panoplied upon the plain;

When snipe are drumming far and near,
And wild flowers fringe the dreaming lode;
Watch the tall rush unsheathe his spear,
The whisper of grey willows hear,
Where once the Briton crushed his woad,
Beside his wattled bleak abode.

Here Saxon fled his Norman lord,
Or hid from the marauding Dane;
Here flashed the steel of Hereward;
The sedge is now the only sword
That waves in all his lost domain;
Come back and dream, O come again.'

The Bird of Hope

BUILD not too high that airy nest of thine,
Far soaring Hope, if thou would'st helpful be;
Though fashioned all with artistry divine—
A golden purpose linked with every line—
It nothing profits where we nothing see;
  The bird that loftiest sings, builds lowliest nest,
  And Hope, that visits heaven, on earth should
    rest.

Else should we know thee but as stars are known,
That move our wonder, but no power impart;
If aught of worth be theirs, 'tis theirs alone,
Each sits a despot on a lonely throne,
Beyond the beat of suffering human heart;
  Hope that avails must come in homelier guise,
  Not clad in splendour of the indifferent skies.

Our lot is cast on an impoverished earth;
War-worn and faint with toil are they that till;
Discouraged are we, questioners of life's worth;
The puny outcome of these days of dearth
Slacks all the tingling fibres of our will.
  Draw near, inspire us, make thy message plain,
  Then, with thee, Bird of Hope, we build again.

'Flu'

ABHORRÈD Influence! Winter's deadliest dart,
The shifting centre of recurring woes!
Thou hast confounded all the doctor's art,
Laying bare the narrow bounds of what he knows.

The red lamps flash, the bottles stand arrayed,
The word goes forth—'The evasive germ is found';
Anon come tidings of foiled ambuscade,
And battle joined on less propitious ground.

Besiege one organ only, storm the heart,
Or take thy station on the seat of pride,
Till our defenders' lumbering batteries start,
They might prevail—would'st thou their brunt abide.

But ever at touch of Aesculapian spear,
(Some daring dose, belike, of deadlier brew,)
Thou feignest flight, while, mustering at the rear,
With Phrygian guile, fresh hosts the fight renew.

So, Protean Horror! multiguised Disease!
Strike where thou wilt, at liver, lung or head;
I stay no parley, pay no useless fees,
But at thy coming, take me to my bed.

A Mountain Harebell

SOME brooding Power from pure ethereal space
Dreamed down its blue, transfiguring as it fell
A formless beauty to thy finished grace,
And draws thee back each dawn from earth's
embrace,
To sound the unfolding hour upon thy bell.

O that our leaden ears were tuned to take
The faint far echoes of that tremulous peal!
To what bright world of wonder should we wake,
If the high thought that moulded thee could make
Life's folded flowers their hidden worth reveal?

Then were we blest as they that hear the beat
Of answering hearts and see love's opening eyes;
Our doubts were dust beneath a dancer's feet,
And songs were ours as when immortals meet,
To acclaim the close of old disharmonies.

An Arran Burn

An hour of singing—and how brave a song!
A score of leaps from thy mossed fountain-
head,
And then, amid wild ocean's crested throng,
Thy form is lost, thy sweet song silenced.

Much is denied thee; none shall track thee down
From prattling shallows to the stately sweep
Of a great river bridged in many a town,
Till age confronts the inevitable deep.

And yet thy voice disdains the note of fear;
Not so they sing who know death glooming by;
Hast thou prevision that experience here
Is but a phase of that which cannot die?

That what falls from thee shall be thine again,
Upgathered where the sun and sea have kissed,
Pledged to return as renovating rain?
Sing on, assured, bright seer and optimist!

Thy song falls charged with solace on an ear
For ever bent to catch what call may be
Beyond a dread sea-sounding, now so near.
Sing on of life reborn, sing on for me!

Midges

RAIDERS from Borderland!
    Scourings of earth and air!
      Your ways are hard to understand,
Your bites are bad to bear.
    With swollen hands my wounds I rub,
    Cursing your god Beëlzebub.

Apollo's burning skies
No terrors held for me,
Till your loathed entry made mine eyes
Go weep like Niobe;
    But now he bends an angered bow,
    As when he laid her offspring low.

Whence come your ravening hordes?
And must we count it true
That, as creation is the Lord's,
There lives some use in you?
    Or may we think from grace ye fell,
    And now are blistering sparks of Hell?

Spoilers of Summer peace!
Prompters of speech profane!
Not till your fell maraudings cease,
Shall I my tongue refrain;
    Till night has stayed your stabs and stings,
    It utters energetic things.

Fiction Old & New

I MOURN the dead disparaged days,
(Victorian that I am)
When Fiction found us saints to praise
And villains dark to damn.

For now the hero sins so deep,
The villain masks so well,
I keep confounding goat with sheep,
And scarce know heaven from hell.

When on the heroine's marble brow
Disfiguring doubts descend,
I feel no glad assurance now
Of smooth harmonious end.

A monied oaf may win the bride,
For whom the hero bled,
And see his rival thrust aside
Duped and discredited.

Or if at last the tangled skein
Is loosed, and love is free,
A funeral knell may gloom the fane
Where marriage bells should be.

And so I praise the naïver days
(Barbarian that I am)
When sinners' souls were set ablaze,
Saints bosomed with Abraham.

Griefs

THERE are some griefs that pass,
    And on their passing, open gates of joy;
    From such come childhood's tears; some
griefs, alas!
Are griefs without alloy.

When a great heart is stilled,
At whose high beat, as at a rallying drum,
A Nation cries: 'We will as thou hast willed,
And at thy call we come.'

While yet that purpose lives,
And moves to its fulfilment, though his grave
Be dewèd with tears, we take what still he gives,
As when he lived and gave.

But when one folly slain,
Sets but another on the dead tyrant's throne,
When he that dies for freedom dies in vain,
Grief then is grief alone.

Pleadings & Verdict

How shall I frame my pleadings, when the deed
    I would be pardoned doing is still to do?
    Doomed innocent Woods!—yet may the
headsman sue,
And his axe fall forgiven, so, hear me plead.

Ye are mine no more; today the bond was sealed,
Tomorrow may despoiling hands be laid
On all your spreading glories; axe and spade
Are sword and spear flashed o'er my lowered shield.

Where I have watched the seasons pass, and seen
Each some excelling gift of beauty bring,
Seen Winter vie with Summer, Fall with Spring;
A ragged waste shall sigh for what has been.

And how shall they that haunt your shadows fare?
What chattering, fluttering fury will there be,
What consternation o'er each crash of tree,
'Mong furry clamberers, outcast singers there!

Yet turn not on me cold accusing eyes;
I soon must follow where you lead the way;
A few swift strokes shall save you from decay,
From age that rots, and lingering, doubly dies.

'Twas Fortune's hand, not mine, prepared the blow,
And but in seeming that my will was there;
Shall I go pardoned hence?—A puff of air
Sends through the wood a shuddering whisper—No!

A Fenland Stream

I KNEW thee first when life was young,
  And scorned thee for thy sauntering pace,
  Called thee a singer with bridled tongue,
A runner that ever had shunned the race.

'If thou wouldst win my praise,' I said,
'And stir my heart, as my native rills,
Bid the sun suck thee from thy bed,
And storm-clouds bear thee to the hills.

Taste there life's thrills, and rapturous leap
From crag to crag in a glory of spray,
Fling loose thy fettered song, and keep
Unsullied all thy channelled way.

No drowsy weeds shall clog thy course,
No serried osiers wall thee round;
There live, a bright embodied force,
Linked ever to a soul of sound.'

But now—too many a change I see
To wish thee other than thou art,
Thy stillness mirrors heaven for me,
And, more than music, feeds my heart.

The Choice

WHEN tossed on summer waves of heat,
   I seek a haven dear to me,
   Where river-arching alders meet,
And gnarled roots form fantastic seat,
   What book shall my companion be?

Shall Science clank her causal chain,
   Till thought in wonder finds release?
As well be at my desk again
As court such buffeting of brain,
   In hours I consecrate to peace.

Loose then your lyric ardour, chase
   Some nimble Georgian's flying feet;
Alas, that were indeed a race
For one who, at a bovine pace,
   Crops only where the grass is sweet.

Choose then some statelier utterance, see
   Grave Pater weave his languorous prose;
A Dryad whispers from her tree,
'There is not room for him and me,
   Here life is simple, wild the rose.'

Thrice foiled, I cast the net again:
　　A sunny wisdom suits the day,
Go, dally with the sage Montaigne,
Or, giving laughter looser rein,
　　Probe the wild wit of Rabelais.

Again that warning whisper low—
　　'These ill consort with pastoral scene,
'Twas theirs to watch life's motley show,
And break the bubbles worldlings blow,
　　With genial mirth or satire keen.'

Seek out a gentler spirit, choose
　　A dainty wit, a feeling heart;
Let Cowper sing of poplared Ouse,
And morals, ere his clouded muse
　　Renounced the solace of her art.

Too trite, or too didactic! So,
　　Once more I set myself to think,
My choice shall be—ah, now I know—
The smooth, innocuous, dreamy flow,
　　And filmy grace of Maeterlinck.

Source and Goal

Calvin, Loyola and Rabelais studied Greek together
at the University of Paris (about 1530)

As when, companioned on a village green,
　　The horse, the goat, the gabbling goose, are
　　seen,
The self-same browse, through differing channels
　drawn,
Transmutes itself to feather, hoof, and horn;

Or as three rivers, from one tract of snow,
Renounce their kinship and contentious flow,
North, South, and East till, symbolling realm and
   throne,
They stir men's hearts as Danube, Rhine, and Rhone;

So three brave spirits at one fountain fed;
Wrote on one scholars' roll their names of dread;
Then flamed apart, as far as mortals may—
Grim Calvin, Loyola, lusty Rabelais.

The Ultra-Modernist Poet

WE tack no more of meaning to our song
   Than clings to motions of a drifting log;
   Form, grammar, rhyme we spurn; such
gauds belong
To simpering bard and brain-drugged pedagogue.

Cut loose from moorings of ancestral thought,
Unruddered by the reason or the will,
Carrying no anchor, for we seek no port,
We view, indifferent, sails that flag or fill.

Enough that, as the tides of feeling pass,
Some trivial moment of the unmeaning flow
Is caught and pinned beneath transfiguring glass,
That we may watch its tortured image glow.

What else is left us? gone are codes and creeds,
And smug conceits that waked Victorian lyres;
Mind is for us a string of worthless beads,
And life a fatuous round of balked desires!

My Pipe

THEY told me,—and a fluttering heart
  Their boding frowns confirms—
  That you and I, my Pipe, must part,
Or I draw near the worms.

So for a joyless year, my Pipe,
I lived estranged from you,
A year I now from memory wipe,
And all its work undo.

For when I laid you thus aside,
My Pipe, I could not know
That in your place a fatuous pride
Would root itself and grow.

I thought of saintly men of old
Who freed their souls from snares,
And told myself, if all were told,
My deed would rank with theirs.

I felt the smug insidious thrill
That conscious virtue knows,
And, O my Pipe! I feel it still,
And shrink from what it shows.

So, at long last, I count the cost,
As victors count the slain,
And lest my very soul be lost,
My Pipe! I smoke again!

Job

WHEN Job upraised him from the dust,
His 'friends' rebuked, his flocks restored,
Returned he to his former trust?
Served he, in thought, a righteous Lord?
  Or, pondering on his causeless pain,
  Turned he to troubling doubts again?

Dark Seer and Bard of long ago,
Where do thy shadowed musings tend?
Designedst thou for thy tale of woe
That all too edifying end?
  Or trace we here the intruding hand
  Of one o'er-quick to understand?

Doubts exiled oft, as oft recur,
Faith falls to questioning while she sings;
Did Job or his accusers err?
Sits Justice at the heart of things?
  Or must man, faltering out his praise,
  Add—'Yet he walks not in our ways'?

Some Similes

I WATCHED a languid apathetic Hern,
(For so he seemed) stand half a summer day,
In the warm shallows of a reed-bound bay,
And not a motion could my eyes discern.
So sat the Buddha 'neath his tamarisk tree,
Waiting for wisdom, steeped in vacancy.

So have I seen within his prison tank
The scaled cadaverous noisome crocodile
Lie, loglike, dreaming of his native Nile—
Of loved malodorous creek or slimy bank.—
I classed him with the Hern, and read in both
Regardless ease, incorrigible sloth.

And both I wronged! As touched by sudden fire,
I saw a lithe neck lashing to and fro,
In deadly sweeps, while each successive blow
Brought wriggling recompense for leashed desire;
And when I lightly tapped a saurian scale,
Wild was the leap that foiled the treacherous tail.

And so, again, impenetrably deep,
May seem the slumber of earth's central fire.
Purged of his vengeful intermittent ire,
Enceladus has settled down to sleep.
Then, with a start he wakes! Resounding woe
Floods all the vine-clad terraces below.

And so, once more, quiescent and resigned,
In the false vision of a tyrant's eye,
By long submission tamed, a Land may lie,
As coveys cower when hawks sail down the wind.
Then something breaks the spell,—there comes a
    day
When thrones are shattered, crowns are cast away!

The Ichthyosaurus

GRIM pirate of the past,
    Pest of a primal sea,
    A vampire laid, stone-coffined, here at last
He sleeps eternally.

He had no foes to fear,
No food to find,
None dared attack him, nutriment was near,
He had no need of mind.

Armed with those awful jaws,
With avid eyes aflame,
He tore and slew at leisure, laughed at laws,
And gloried in his shame,

Indulging every whim,
Fell sybarite of the sea,
But Nemesis had spread a net for him—
He died of sheer ennui!

The Lost Mammalian Eye

WHEN Nature sifted out our eyes
From cruder visual stuff,
She felt a troubling doubt arise
If two would prove enough.

So, on the head's unfeatured rear,
A third incipient eye
Was made, but made to disappear;
Why? Ye Darwinians! Why?

How came that proudly prescient Mind
To strangle at its birth
A form that, functioning behind,
Had vast 'survival worth'?

When chased about, where motors meet,
And Death stands gaping by,
I mourn, while terror wings my feet,
That lost aborted eye.

o—< 19 >—o

Had not blind folly cancelled it,
Life had been still astir,
Where now the questing jury sit,
Around their coroner.

The Nightingale & Her Rivals

MISDEEM not, Priestess of the voice divine!
Praise of another's song dispraise of thee;
The poets of all ages deck thy shrine,
Thou hast the full libation of their wine,
What profit were there, wert thou praised of me?
  Thy place is where immortal singers are;
  Be thou their moon, but let me praise a star.

Then hear, magnanimous, that as pure a note
As ever thou on midnight air didst pour,
Has found a passage through the Throstle's throat,
And sounds at eve where, clad in sable coat,
The Blackbird tells his trouble o'er and o'er;
  Thine ampler theme yields more sustained delight
  Yet these make glad the day, as thou the night.

O let me think thou lend'st a pleasured ear
To rival song, when bright hours hold thee mute,
Too high thy glory sits for envious fear,
Thou art no jealous Sun-god, joyed to hear
Poor Marsyas moaning by his conquered flute,
  No Muse triumphant, spurning from her knees,
  In pitiless pride, the lost Pierides.

The Ostrich

(A new parry for an old thrust)

POOR butt of ignorant scorn from days of yore!
　　Pictured head-hiding in the desert sand;
　　He never wanted wits, nor used them more
Than in that ruse men so misunderstand.

His long white neck he neatly tucks away,
Erects his leaf-like plumes, and seems to be—
To the bamboozled eyes of beasts of prey—
The desert-dotting bush or stunted tree.

Unhappy Bird! derided, mocked, maligned,
As mindless, for his plainest proof of mind!

Bard & Bee

'She gathers honey all the day
From every opening flower.'

FLOWERS brew not honey, Bard! protests the
　　Bee;
　　From their crude lymph our patient toil dis-
　　tilled
The drop that shames their art; and not by thee,
O Bard, is all men praise thee for fulfilled.

Thou art the flower the luring drop prepares
For after-handling by some abler bee,
For never poet yet was found who dares
To say 'My honey owes its all to me.'

So, through the web man's thought essays to spin,
Some threads of purpose wind their conscious way,
But soon undreamed of patterns form within,
As though unbidden fingers were at play.

Whose that dark weaving, what the up-welling
    power,
We know no more than knows the honey-bee
Who calls her forth to raid the expectant flower,
And guides her to her goal unerringly.

An East Wind

WE have no tears to spare
    For foiled ambition, writhing in his chains,
    For greed, lamenting his diminished gains,
For sordid sorrow, and ignoble care;
These do but reap the harvest of their pains.

But when young hearts have given
Their all for peace, and on their graves have grown
Pale blossoming hopes, and then, O then, has blown
An east wind blighting all and shrouding heaven,
Our tears fall fitly where those flowers are strown.

The Whale

HAD Earth no welcome for thee when possessed
    By some dim yearning, thou, with myriads
        more
Thy sea-born fellows, fled'st the wave's unrest,
To cast thy fortunes on the forming shore?

All crept from out the deep when earth was mire,
The same blind impulse ever urging on;
Each upward step brought sight of fresh desire,
One hope fulfilled, another fairer shone.

They took strange shapes to fit their various life,
As heeding Nature's call 'Adapt or die';
Fashioned rude arms for multifarious strife,
Roamed utmost earth, or plumed them for the sky;

And none looked back but thou, and thou hast
   shared
Her fate who, bidden from Jahveh's wrath to flee,
Gave backward glance where guilty Sodom flared,
She turned to salt, and thou returned'st to sea.

To My Sub-Liminal Self

How came we thus together?
   Dark Spirit housed in me!
   Bound by what fatal tether
Closer than claw to feather,
Or flower to honey-bee?

Thou wak'st when I am sleeping,
Ousting me from my throne,
My past lies in thy keeping,
I spend long hours in reaping
The tares thy hand has sown.

A sage that oft will blunder,
A saint that stoops to shame,
In all thy ways a wonder,
Thou rendest life asunder,
And I must bear the blame.

When I am tuned to sadness,
Thou unabashed wilt play,
But in thy ribald gladness
Confusion lives, and madness
Is never far away.

Wilt thou be standing by me,
In Heaven's all-judging day,
Pleading with them that try me,
Or wilt thou then deny me,
And go thy separate way?

The Loveless Sea

THE Deep that lieth under
Spake to the realms above—
My works abound in wonder,
But yours are crowned with love.

Trust not that legend hoary,
Love rose not from the sea,
In heaven she sits in glory,
O'er earth she wanders free;

But through my wastes of water
Her footsteps never stray,
Though seas run red with slaughter,
She chides not them that slay.

I nursed Life's rude beginnings,
On earth transformed they grow,
To count among their winnings
The love I ne'er may know.

There e'en the tigress-mother
Will die, her young to save,
Heaven's birds love one another,
Nought loves beneath the wave.

Kindly Death

DEATH never came in tenderer guise,
 Nor wore a milder mien,
 Than when he sealed those loving eyes,
And blanched that brow serene.
 He stilled the beating of his wing,
 That she might hear the angels sing.

All gently did he disengage
Life's essence from its earthly dress,
And from the withered husk of age
Drew forth its inner loveliness,
 To waft it on his pinions wide
 To where God's saintliest souls abide.

We thank thee for that reverent hand,
O kindly Death! when deep thy share
Drives through a desolated land,
Unveil that look we saw thee wear,
 When, all thy terrors laid aside,
 Thou cam'st the friend, the heavenward guide.

The Trapped Squirrel

As though the hand that sets him free
Had been behind his whole mishap,
He meets his chattering teeth in me,
As part or partner of the trap;
And seems to boast, though both are bit,
He has the last and best of it.

Released, in scurrying haste he hies
To where, a braggart hero, he
Recounts, with bright dilated eyes,
To furry ears, his fight with me;
Of biter bitten he tells, and tit
For tat, and all the rest of it.

For me, whose pity-prompted deed
Has met with such a fierce rebuff,
Though fast the officious finger bleed,
The accomplished good is good enough;
The deed and doom may badly fit,
But justice makes a jest of it.

If well and ill directed aim
Found each its due requital here,
Life were for most a duller game,
Though played in saintlier atmosphere;
If chance defeat and lucky hit
Were gone, gone were the zest of it.

The Neanderthal Man

OF your wild blood no drop is ours,
    Remote Mousterian Man—
    You of the simian brow that lowers
O'er eyes of Caliban.

Yet something in you spurned the brute,
    In moments rare and brief,
Some sap was bubbling at the root
    That never reached the leaf.

You lived begirt by grisly foes,
    Death ever crouching near,
Yet left no record of your woes,
    But many a trace of cheer.

How came it, then, you missed the road
    That leads to 'Sapient Man'?
What horror stormed your bleak abode,
    And tracked you when you ran?

O many have gone the way you went,
    And myriads more must go,
Ere, Nature's fund of fancy spent,
    Form triumphs over flow.

The Crocodile's Apologia

WHEN vital power, emerging from the mud,
    Judged that experience here was worth its
      while,
It fell to fashioning forms of flesh and blood,
And made, in cynic mood, a crocodile.

It took discarded remnants left behind
By the first failures, botched them anyhow,
Threw in a dash of rudimentary mind,
Then laughed to see me as you see me now!

You call me earth's disgrace, reproach of heaven,
A loathsome horror, greedy, treacherous, vile.
Well, well! tut, tut! we live by what is given,
And my best gifts were cunning, greed, and guile.

Where were the wings wherewith I might have
    flown?
Could I dispense with ravening teeth and jaws,
When means to loftier life were all unknown?
Why gird at consequence, and skip the cause?

If beauty goes as deep as goes the skin,
With hide like mine there should be much in me;
If the contractor failed to work it in,
The blame is his though mine the penalty.

Had you been cradled in a river-bed,
And I climbed ever under fortune's smile,
Which had been then the form that forged ahead?
I had been you, and you—a crocodile!

The Lost Chance

T HERE came a Chance, that on me bent the
        fire
    Of eager, questioning eyes,
Searching my soul if haply there desire
Burned still for enterprise;

If still lay drowsed within me power to break
From harboured, anchored ease,
And winged with purpose, follow in the wake
Of venturous argosies.

O lost and forlorn Chance! The power was there,
The power, but not the will;
One pulse of shamed endeavour shook the air,
And all again was still.

I did but loose the shadow of a sigh
From lips that now, in vain,
Ask each cloud-wanderer from an alien sky—
When comes that Chance again?

On Hanging up the Vanes of an Aeroplane

HERE let them hang, that oft have hung in air,
To flash, with following thunder, on the foe;
Here let them rest, that knew no resting there,
Till warped and withered like the beams around
   they grow.

As dinted armour decks ancestral hall,
And war-worn memoried ensigns droop and fade
In vaulted aisle, so shall these vanes recall
Deeds till our days undreamed of, in high heaven
   essayed.

These have adventured where no eagle yet
Has raised exulting plume, ay, far away,
Beyond earth's straining vision, have they met
A lonely challenge to a dread unwitnessed fray.

No trumpet pealed the signal for the fight,
(To many a deadly brunt these wings have flown)
No plaudits rose, that nerve the charging knight,
Where he that ruled their fury fought aloft, alone.

And ne'er was honour grudged to foe that fell
Before the rushing of these victor vanes,
Whose measured throb beat out his dying knell;
No deed that earth defiled the air's proud record
    stains.

Fortune's Web

FORTUNE's web Man may not break,
    Yet has he helped to weave;
    What she has given, he must take,
What she denies him, leave;
    Yet in these bounds he finds him scope
    For fruitful toil and endless hope.

Faint that spark of heavenly fire
Man counts it his to tend,
Yet 'twill avail to burn desire,
That may not heavenward bend,
    And in its faithful tendance lies
    The hope and measure of his rise.

Chafe not that the end is far,
Nor that the light is dim,
That end is where the angels are,
That light crowns seraphim;
    Man rose from out the deeps, and yet
    To that high bourn his course is set.

Man and His Dwelling-Place

A PUPPET pulled by hidden string,
    Or centre of experienced power;
    Immortal spirit, or a thing
That casts its case, to buzz and sting,
And die forgotten in an hour;
  Which part is man's?—They best can say,
  Who make the most of what they may.

A world by Love and Wisdom planned,
Or swirl in ether, speck in space;
The hollow of a Father's hand,
Or cowering spot 'mid desert sand:
Which pictures best man's dwelling-place?
  They best have known, who most have striven,
  Whate'er that home, to make it heaven.

The Last Abbot

(Hanged on Glastonbury Tor, 1538)

H E watched the sowing of the wind
    That to a whirlwind grew,
    And saw the impetuous reaper bind
Old faith with ordinance new.

The shadow of a monstrous hand,
Outstretched for loot and prey,
Moved, a black storm-cloud, o'er the land
To where the great abbey lay.

He hears denouncing thunder sound,
And meets the lightning's eye,
And soon, dishonoured, mocked and bound,
They lead him forth to die.

He leaves in baser keeping now
St Joseph's holy thorn,
But feels its impress on his brow,
As when it once was worn;

And high above his wasted shrine,
Where all he ruled might see,
He tasted of the bitter wine
They brewed on Calvary.

Though all he loved lies shattered round,
His thorn bears blossom still,
And still they count it holy ground
Who mount the martyr's hill.

Mrs Thomas Atkins

THE Spring has called the catkins
And the catkins call the bee,
And Corporal Thomas Atkins
Has been to call on me.

It's little Corporal Atkins cares
For tassels on a tree,
He wastes no thought on such, but swears
He's thinking much of me.

It's only for its honey
That he cares about the bee,
He cares much more for money,
And most of all for me.

He did not sing the praise of Spring,
But in the nicest way,
He said the very sort of thing
I hoped he'd come to say.

He did not beat about the bush,
Like some who come to woo,
But carried matters with a rush,
As soldiers ought to do.

He hoped, he said, to get a rise
And be a sergeant soon,
And then he took my finger's size
And planned the honey-moon.

So the Spring may call the catkins,
And the catkins call the bee,
But you'll call me Mrs Atkins,
When next you call on me.

The World of Sense

HAD we one sense the more,
Our past were worlds away,
And we, like sailors skirting a savage shore,
Might watch a rude race at their barbarous play,
Nor know them for ourselves of yesterday.

Had we one sense the less,
A shrunken earth were ours,
Though we, like plants in sun-scorched wilderness,
That turn to roots their outer pendent flowers,
Transformed might thrive, nor mourn our vanished
    powers.

Of sense our world we build,
Unsensed 'twould cease to be,
And yet we trust, when all has been fulfilled,
And shows are sundered from reality,
Beyond this world of sense new worlds to see.

A Cambridge Plaint

As though the flame-heart, ribbed and cased
          with steel,
          Of some sea-shouldering monster were
athrob;
As though vast cauldrons for Gargantuan meal
With rhythmed fury shook on giant hob;
Once more, as though a dread reverberate drum
Stirred Afric's hordes to deeds of devildom;

So through the length of each September day,
To those whom Fate holds in sad durance here,
With the malignant thud of waves that prey
Upon a writhing beach, there stuns the ear,
That fain would fill with siren-baffling wax,
The thunderous Beat of Carpets on 'The Backs.'

Chance & Change

To the chance reading of a book,
          Or flash of some remembered scene,
          Some silent sufferer's upward look,
Or thought of things that might have been—
          To this or that, in after days,
          We trace the parting of the ways.

Yet ne'er was Fate, or wandering Chance
     Sole lord of that uplifting hour;
The passing touch of circumstance
     But loosed some hidden spring of power;
          And whatsoever foes we front,
          That inward power must bear the brunt.

Threshed Out

THE chaff lay thick on the threshing floor,
    The grain had gone to mill,
    Yet men there came who threshed it o'er,
And some are threshing still.

They strove new meanings to extort
    From what before was plain,
And, when their labour came to naught,
    They threshed it all again.

Strange pranks they played with mood and tense,
    A livelier tale to tell,
And, when conjecture yielded sense,
    They judged that all was well.

In many a rifled treasure-house,
    They found the nest of mare;
They tracked the labouring-mountain mouse
    Back to his secret lair.

They cast about for cryptic sign
    Of esoteric lore,
Though meaning clear as morning shine,
    They prove it clouded o'er.

The bending of a solemn brow
    A saddening sight must be,
When every furrow speaks of plough,
    That ploughs or sand or sea.

O wild excess of ponderous toil!
    O weary waste of skill!
All scant and meagre is the spoil,
    Yet are they threshing still.

A Rebuke

I DID but oust you from the chair
  I most affect when toil is ended,
  And with Zenobia's outraged air
By Caesar's car, you sit offended;
    If thoughts of Cats can e'er be read,
    Yours may be thus interpreted—

Because it makes for warmth and ease
To hold a hearth and home in common,
You think to lord it as you please,
You made the same mistake with Woman;
    And one who, when admonished once,
    Repeats his fault, is dubbed a dunce!

Man's part is plain—to pay the rent,
Tend fires, and superintend the rations,
And minister to Cats' content
By muzzling dogs and bridling passions;
    To play the blustering autocrat
    Makes no impression on a Cat.

'Tis like your blunderings in the East
With older, more reposeful races,
You shift your moods till man or beast,
Cuffed, petted, spoiled, kicks o'er the traces;
    (I do not kick, of course, for that
    Were unbecoming in a Cat.)

So, by renowned Osirian Nile,
Where once your race was held in reverence,
You helped lame dogs o'er many a stile,
And hear them yelping now for severance;
    Had you but owned our air serene,
    You had been gods—as Cats have been.

Pause ere your folly drives more deep,
'Tis manners mostly call for mending;
Let Cats and tired Nations sleep,
Keep pert officials from offending;
    Then East and West, and Cats and Men
    May be the best of friends again.

The Explorers

WE blame him not who counts it blest
    To prove his powers on dangerous quest—
    Who stands on airless Everest,

Or steels the sinews of his soul
To front the fiends that guard the Pole,
Or takes some Mecca for his goal;

Who wings it to the verge of air,
Or tracks the lion to his lair—
These know their danger. Let them dare!

More venturous he, and more unwise,
Who turns, untrained, his questing eyes
On inward deeps and mysteries,

Intent to drag to light of day
Some slumbering, dark, ancestral trait,
From conscious life long locked away.

Pure must his mind and purpose be,
Who of that chamber turns the key,
And can, with soul unsullied, see;

For twisted truths and errors crass
Lurk in those deeps, like snakes in grass,
With power to poison all who pass.

As when some rifler of the tomb
Of king accurst shapes in the gloom
Some shadowy minister of doom,

Unblest, discarded shreds of mind,
That mounting life has left behind,
Aroused, may fresh vocation find,

And they who to such haunts repair,
To lay some guilt or folly bare,
May know contamination there.

Let those alone these perils face,
Whose healing hands are skilled to trace
The dark complexities of race.

The Seasons

I ASKED no more of Autumn than a sigh
For Summer dead, and with a sigh she came,
But of such healing air its passing by
Stirred Summer's ashes to a living flame;
And the twin seasons sang—'There is no death
While beauty lives and love remembereth.'

I asked of Winter, bowed beneath his snows,
And racked by storms, how he sustained his fate;
His winds brought answer—'From my cloudy woes
Tears for Earth's healing I precipitate;
Where, without Winter, were the smiles of Spring?
Where, without sorrow, joy in anything?'

The River Manifold

(Which takes an underground course between Wetton Mill
and Ilam Hall in Dovedale)

WHAT found ye wanting here?
Ye languished, ebbing waters! Round you
    lies
Earth's beauty as it broke on Adam's eyes;
Music ye added fit for an angel's ear,
Yet as in thirsting sands ye waste, or desert drear.

As though in sick disdain
Of all that gave your strength and beauty birth,
And fed your song, ye plunge in caverned earth,
Threading the darkness like a molten vein,
Till, with a vast upheave, ye front the stars again,

Where Ilam rears her towers,
Ringed round and shadowed deep with ashen grove,
As when the courtly Congreve loved to rove,
And tune his wit where ye made bright his bowers,
Ere fashion's smooth deceits laid waste his youthful
    powers.

Thou dost but do as they,
Fair Stream! who, shrinking from encounter rude,
Steep their embittered souls in solitude,
Till their forbidden music ebbs away,
And brows are swathed in gloom that might have
    borne the bay.

May these win back, as thou,
The light forsaken and the song forsworn,
That in their age, some grace youth might have worn
May break like blossom on a sullen bough,
That long has idly hung, and seems all sapless now.

Soundings

M AN at his peril probes, yet probe he must,
To find a firm foundation for the trust
That mingles with the cloudings of his dust.

Deep through the common clay life's lowliest share
He digs, to find his doubts have dogged him there;
When his last soundings cease, no rock lies bare.

Abandoning earth, he meets with bold surmise
The challenge flashed from night's unnumbered eyes,
And shapes a Whole, where contradiction dies.

That dream dissolved, he turns his gaze within,
And shuddering sees a sombre dawn begin
With implications of the sense of sin.

The Puff-Adder

O N thy loathed form a problem hangs,
How came so vile a thing to be,
If quivering hate and venomed fangs
Owe not their birth to devilry?
Was each foul trait a thought divine,
Or was the dark imagining thine?

Was all decreed, no chance, no choice,
No mingling of a 'may' with 'must,'
But Doom's inexorable voice—
'Brew death, and lurk in desert dust,'
Or, ere the shaping hand was still,
Was nature marred by chosen ill?

If thou couldst urge that in thee lies
The seed of better things to be,
We might offset thy future rise
Against thy present infamy;
But who has ever found a trace
In thee of supervenient grace?

So we must darkly ponder still,
What broods behind thy baleful hiss,
Or shape, as sundry sophists will,
Some specious, soothing synthesis,
And, to exonerate Nature, prove
Hate is but undeveloped love!

Dream-Plots

WHAT eyes are those that darkly see
When outward sense is laid asleep?
And what those ears where sound for me
Wild ravings of some inner deep?—
For more than pictured memories rise,
And echoes, to those ears and eyes.

Who fashions in those teeming hours
Dark plots, incriminating speech;
Exalting passion till it towers
Beyond its utmost waking reach,
And with the pilfered tools of sense
Builds Bedlams—Who is he, and whence?

Exile

Not ours the peaks that lift on high
A Titan's heaven-assailing spear,
In air so pure the questioning eye
No measure finds of far or near;
   Yet our low fells the enchantment yield
   Of beauty veiled and half-revealed.

No torrent ours, whose clouded flow
The secret of its source betrays,
In cheerless wastes of weltering snow;
Its furious course let others praise;
   But ours the streamlets crystal-clear,
   That lose themselves in Windermere.

I watch a tideless water make
A glory of its winter spray,
Alas! that scene so fair should wake
Wild wish to be where, far away,
   A shallow, shimmering, soundless sea
   Steals o'er a sand-strewn estuary.

Dolce far Niente

Long crushed beneath a leaden crown,
   Earth draws today such radiance down,
   Its flooding glory dims the line
Where earth-born beauty meets divine,
Till homing angels scarce could know
Heaven from its counter-part below.

The call of such consummate day
I may not, dare not, disobey,
And till its ardours shall abate
I hold its peace inviolate,
In cool grey deeps of willowed shade,
Where waters move and songs are made.

'Neath tangled lashes eyes of blue,
Outposts of heaven, are peering through,
And till they burn with starry fire,
I fill my coffers of desire,
For here each affluent hour of day
Its passing toll in peace shall pay.

Lest joy should fail from sheer excess,
I court a prudent passiveness,
Deputing to bird, flower, and tree
Vicarious power to act for me.

Would I thank heaven for such a day,
The lark shall sing what I would say,
Or, for an envoy grave, I turn
To yon staid reverential hern;
While honey-blooms that cluster by
Burn incense for me to the sky,
And on the sun-charged odorous air
Float droning orisons everywhere.

Does the full heart demand a tear,
Are there not weeping-willows here?
Its rhythmed beat shall tune its speed
By yon slow wavering water-weed;
Its prisoned yearnings find their vent
In sedge-fowl flutings of content,
While the bent osiers' gentle stir
Shall be my soul's interpreter.

Thought! urge no more those labouring wings,
Plumed with unquiet questionings;
Sleep! break that half-spun web, for where
In thy dim world is dream so fair?
And Memory! till yon sun has set,
Be merciful, I would forget.

Thus, opening all the pores of sense,
I trap each passing influence,
While in the circle of the soul,
The part expands to meet the whole;
And till high heaven draws back its blue,
With sap of nature thrilling through,
I share in all, yet nothing do.

Identity

IF it so chanced that to my soul there came
Another, point to point equipped the same,
By the same dreams inspired of fear and hope,
Its motions ruled by powers of equal scope,
Drawn by like aims to the same far-off end,
Would my soul with that other's being blend?

Since life is doing, and like deeds are done,
Would these twin agents integrate as one,
The supervening essence merge in mine,
As shattered star will with its shatterer shine?
Or dare I think some inmost core of me
Repels transfusion through eternity?

Gleam & Eddy

By passion urged and pain,
  Through fields of promise, thick with error
    sown,
Groping and stumbling, every sense astrain,
Life's children rose and fell, and rose again,
Till each had found the form he fain would own.

Then, in dulled eyes, the gleam,
All once had followed, flickered down and died;
Caught in some changeless eddy of Life's stream,
His fevered past a lost, discarded dream,
Each in the form he fashioned must abide.

Man only, born as they,
Treading where they had trodden, custom bound,
But custom-breaking, keeps the upward way,
And through Life's tangle sees the fitful ray
That points him past that eddy's fateful round.

But, envious of the lot
Of his unchanging fellows freed from care,
Weary of strivings these have long forgot,
Sick of vague yearnings for he knows not what,
Man oft has seen that gleam dissolve in air.

A Garden Tragedy

I ran to save—ran as I rarely run,
  But in a flash the abhorrèd deed was done,
  A life was ended and a meal begun!

Distasting scenes, betwixt himself and me
He judged it well to interpose a tree,
There, since I could no other, I let him be.

With barbarous ritual, passionless and grim,
As some grave doom-denouncing Sanhedrim,
He tore my luckless Robin limb from limb.

Calm and deliberate, observant of laws
That frown on haste and eager wolfing jaws,
He ate with languorous ease and frequent pause.

The session closed, he turned and met my gaze,
With a proud purr, as though expecting praise
For deftly demonstrating Nature's ways.

Making a pulpit of a neighbouring mound,
I set his sin before him in phrases round;
He should have been abased, but did abound!

The Maestro

WITH anxious care we set the stage
        For Thought, the master-singer here;
        But who that knows him dare engage
That, on our call, he will appear;
        For oft our hopes expectant wait,
        And disappointed, dissipate.

We know not from what hidden deep
    Thought rises to our conscious day,
Nor when, like phantom forms of sleep,
    On near approach, he will away,
        While his faint footfall leaves behind
        Dull echoes in an empty mind.

And are they ours—those songs he sings?
　　Or come they from a loftier sphere?
Away with idle questionings!
　　And reverent rise—the master's here,
　　　　And till departure breaks the spell
　　　　Of Thought's high witchery, all is well.

Bickerings

THE Soil said to the Seed—
　　'All that thou hast of worth, or hop'st to be,
　　All that shall part thee from the veriest weed,
Comes as a gift from me.'

The Sower said to the Soil—
'My help withheld, what would thy gifts avail?
Thou dost but set the scene where skill and toil
Make good what else must fail.'

The Seed made answer—'Peace!
Base thralls that on my outward state attend,
Within me lies the power that works increase,
Means are ye, I am end.'

The Sun o'erheard their strife,
And with a laugh that rocked the firmament,
'Ye do but trim,' said he, 'the lamp of life,
Which I, life's lord, have lent;

From me all power proceeds,
My bounty gives whatever gifts are given,
Source of all life, and doer of all deeds,
I drive, all else are driven.'

None dared to make reply,
Or ask how came such potency to birth,
But one far luminary's awful eye
Brimmed o'er with twinkling mirth.

Treason

I HEARD Life's inmost Lord complain—
These traitors round my throne,
Dull Flesh and ever-plotting Brain,
Miscall my powers their own.

Last of a line of phantom kings,
The Soul, they say, shall fall;
There is no heaven-built heart of things,
A law-bound earth is all.

When I am most inspired to serve
A purpose high and good,
They say some twitching web of nerve
Provokes exuberant blood!

And when a more than earthly peace
Is by Heaven's favour sent,
Some famished function wins release,
Through new-found nourishment!

My loneliest deeps the irreverent crew
Probe with an impious hand,
To prove that all I seem to do
Is done at their command.

But now that Death stands beckoning there,
I heed these levellers less,
For howsoe'er the Soul may fare,
Their fate is nothingness.

A Wild Flower Catechized

ART thou the more a flower that to mine eyes
     Thou seem'st so fair?
     Of thy sweet essence lives there aught that
dies,
When I, thy lover, am no longer there?
Was all thy beauty showered thee from the skies,
Or in its moulding had my heart a share?
When of that beauty others have their will,
Art thou the more a flower, and fairer still?

The Four Pilgrims

FOUR pilgrims crouched in gloom before the gate
     That guards the precincts of eternal day;
     Aloof they cowered, bemoaning each his fate,
Nor had they been companions on the way.

Each had essayed to enter, each had known
The pang of cold repulse, he wist not why;
Each had brought gifts to lay before the throne
Of Him who thus their access did deny.

One bore a banner, on it 'Truth' was writ
In fiery blazon. 'From my youth,' he cried,
'I sought for knowledge, found and followed it;
Truth led me living, and for Truth I died.'

One, helmed, with jewelled crest that gleamed afar
Above his troubled visage, made lament,
'I took bright Beauty for my guiding star,
And bore her gage through life's rough tournament.'

The third, in deep dejection, beat his breast
And made fierce moan, 'I would,' he cried, 'be free,
Of man's high attributes I chose the best,
I toiled and fought and died for Liberty.'

Last, one of sterner aspect bowed his head
In saddened wonder, and reproachful spoke—
'I strove for Right and Order, both are dead
If I stand doomed, that never ordinance broke.'

Each note in sorrow's diapason thus
Was sounded till the whole sad theme was clear,
Then rose one cry—'God has forsaken us,
One fate is ours, why stand we strangered here?'

So draw they each to other, hand with hand
Is joined, when lo! the gates of heaven unbar,
And answer comes—'O slow to understand,
One common fault your pilgrimage did mar,

One fault alone, each else has nobly striven,
Why came ye singly here? This made your sin,
Truth, Order, Beauty, Freedom know not heaven,
Till linked by Love; rise now and enter in.'

The Fens

So deep our thirst for heaven,
   We suffer not one rude upthrusting height
   To break its blue, or blot the glory given,
But, prostrate and adoring, drink delight.

No tract of polar sea,
Or surf-encircled equatorial shore,
Owns ampler store of starry bliss than we,
Or glories in its ringed horizon more.

Time moves with plodding pace,
Meeting no check, no challenge, on his way;
And wherefore should he speed, when idle Space
With outstretched limbs lies dreaming all the day?

Storms that had spread alarm
Through peopled shires, or robbed a realm of peace,
Rage idly here till, awed by the solemn calm
On all things round, they whimper, sigh and cease.

But for man's guiding hand,
That led blind erring waters to the sea,
That sea were never found, but with the land
Were mixed and weltered all confusedly.

In the old days of fear,
This reed-bound refuge from the abounding woe
Bred saint and hero, legends linger here
Of broken peoples and the black-ravened foe.

And in these days of stress,
When red confusion riots in our dreams,
Thou still canst soothe, O Land of Loneliness!
Of the long levels and the slow unsounding streams.

Armenia

WERE all thy blood and tears upgathered
round thee,
Thou wert as Pharaoh, whelmed in a
redder sea;
Thy foes were ours, we loosed the chains that
bound thee,
And pledged our common faith thou shouldst
be free.

Thy still un-rainbowed Ararat before thee
Stands a reproach to Heaven for what has been;
The dove went forth, but still the waters o'er thee
Fling their cold spray, no ransomed earth is seen.

The oppressor bowed beneath our haughty chiding,
With eastern guile; we let the occasion go;
Ours was the fitful purpose, his the abiding:
The steadfast hate that feeds on coming woe.

Men's thoughts are far from thee; fear, greed and
    sorrow
Hold down the West, whence only help could come;
Ears filled with muttering thunders of tomorrow
Are deaf, and lips that bade thee hope are dumb.

Not thine alone, O lost abandoned nation!
The star that sinks beneath a reddening wave;
Thy foes shall tread the path of tribulation,
Thy friends shall mourn dishonoured by thy grave.

The Measured Arc

FATE may decide what buffets thou shalt meet,
But how thou meetest them is thine alone;
There may thy soul be spilt, and there defeat
May prove the dark soil where best grain is grown.

Though ruined earth be all thy heritage,
Whose tilling may thine utmost power exceed,
Still may thy toil its bitterness assuage,
Thy soul draw strength from each uprooted weed.

Earth's wisest know their wisdom's narrow bounds,
Strength in her strongest is a little thing,
Her harmonies to Heaven's are jarring sounds,
Yet do they well who ponder, toil and sing.

Each thus his measured arc of being bends,
To shape the full-ringed glory none may see
(Save in rapt vision) till time's frustrate ends
Find their fulfilment in eternity.

Erin (1920)

MANY love thee whom thou hatest, Erin,
For thy dreary griefs of long ago;
On thy brow sits furrowed anger, Erin;
Must it be for ever so?

Like the glamours on thy mountains, Erin,
Mists have guiled those dark averted eyes,
Facts distorting, friend with foe confounding;
May we never see them rise?

Linked with us in many a proud tradition,
Wielding with us wide imperial sway,
Still the shadow looms between us, Erin;
Will it never pass away?

Earth has bitter need of helping, Erin,
And there is help in that sad heart of thine;
Turn thy tears to drops of healing, Erin;
And through them let a new forgiveness shine.

E'en the red hand of aliened Ulster, Erin,
May yet be thine, if thine the will to be
Gracious in giving, as stubborn in defending,
The freedom dear to others as to thee.

O long oppressed! scorn thou to be the oppressor;
Let thy vain dream of isolation go;
E'en as we plead, thy dark eyes mock us, Erin;
Must it be for ever so?

OUT of the mists of Erin's mournful mountains
Comes a low rippling laugh, a weary sigh—
'Is it England, with her righteous mood upon
    her,
Sees me weep, and would be wondering why?

Sees me mock the stiff ungainly motion
Of her coldly proffered, long withholden hand,
As, with solemn bending brows of admonition,
She prates of what she cannot understand.

'Tis not memories, England, only stand between us
Of power misused in a barbarian day;
Things you count your present pride, your latest
    glory,
Are the very things we wish away.

Boast to others of your far dominion,
The sordid, guilty splendour of your dreams;
Homelier hopes find echoes on our mountains,
And send a sweeter music down our streams.

When another heart beats in you, England,
And through others' eyes you learn to see,
When you speak as nation speaks to nation,
Come again and ask the hand of me.'

A Lost Home

ONCE more among the mountains! once again
I see my lost home glimmering far away,
Framed by dark woods;—now, with a flush
of rain,
The glimpse has gone, and memories only stay.

Thought follows thought of days that there were
spent,
And, like a silken pageant, sparkled by;
Was ever sorrow there, it came and went
But as a light cloud flecks a summer sky.

'Twas there were woven dreams time turned to
naught,
Hopes there were nourished that have time defied,
There Nature stretched a hand to stumbling thought,
And smoothed the path for joys that yet abide.

That beauty-girdled home knows beauty still,
Though all that made it home for me has gone,
Still red with rusting heather is the hill,
Blue still the mountain peak of Coniston.

Still age-worn alders guard my sleeping mere,
My woodlands wave their welcome as of old,
But gone are they whose life once centred here,
Nor may there be re-gathering to the fold.

Respite

FATE has o'erlooked so many an offered chance
Of ending all that sums itself in Me,
So turned aside the shafts of circumstance,
That wonder asks—Why smiles she thus on thee?

Can hope still linger that an age-worn will,
A slumberer at its post, may wake and find
Redeeming office it may yet fulfil,
Cleansing some weed-choked channel of the mind;

And from the unprisoned effluence wring the power
To trace an ordering whole in bickering parts,
To see the dawn behind the darkest hour,
And weigh the treasure locked in homeliest hearts?

On Receiving a New Weed Poison Warranted to Kill Nettles

I COME as came Queen Eleanor
To Rosamund the Fair,
To tell thee death draws near thy door,
And speed his entry there;
    For, like that termagant, I give
    What makes it difficult to live.

Earth counts thee meanest of her flowers,
The sorriest weed that grows,
Yet art thou armed with deadlier powers
Than guard the regal rose;
    But Science lifts a poisoned spear;
    Feel, if thou ever feelest, fear!

Oft have I urged in eager strife
Spud, spade and sickle keen,
All have been levelled at thy life,
Yet left that life serene;
   Like the gross knight, I see thee slain,
   And unabashed rise up again.

But now thine arts avail no more,
As with the treacherous king,
Who met his doom at Elsinore,
The stinger feels the sting;
   He in a garden stung, as thou,
   And Hamlet needs no prompter now.

Salvage

IF ebbing powers so far should fail and fade
  That the sense-world for me were all unmade,
  And it were given me, from the engulfing deep
One cherished scene, one sound, alone to keep,
Of all that ever drew my heart from me;
What would that vision, and what that music be?

Swift were my choice—in exiled hungering eyes,
Lone heathered uplands, once my own, should rise,
And o'er them float the curlew's quavering call;
That scene, that sound, recaptured should atone for
  all.

An Anticipated Judgment

THREE forest queens, each fairest of her kind,
        Would have me play the stale Parisian game;
        But turmoiled heaven, burnt Ilium, rose to
    mind;
Why should I set the topless woods aflame?

Each has her crown: the Elm unequalled height,
The grey-boled Beech consummate curving grace,
Oak outstretched arms that welcome air and light;
Why should I feed insatiate pride of place?

If judge I must, importunately pressed,
Let skilled assessors prompt my faltering powers;
Hale me some feathered Daniel from his nest,
Some petalled Portia from your ambient flowers;

Their judgment shall be mine. While thus I spoke,
I turned an inquisitorial eye on each.
A meaning smile suffused the prescient Oak;
Elm-Hera changed wry looks with Pallas-Beech.

Then, with such scorn as fits the high and mighty,
They left me with an acorned Aphrodite.

A Nocturne

WHERE the lilies dream afloat,—
        Lilies golden, lilies white,—
        The moon's dark mirror bears my boat,
And lingering there, I drink delight
From all the witching moods of night.

Lulling music fills my ear,—
Music low, and music sweet,—
From the muffled plash of weir,
And from where two runlets meet
In rippling concord, at my feet.

By the lilied waters' edge—
Lilied white and lilied gold—
I lie till light airs in the sedge
Whisper that night's tale is told,
And bid the dreaming flowers unfold.

The Wasp That Was

FROM life in three-dimensioned space,
He drops to death in two;
Flat as unruffled ocean's face,
Or flat as falls a common-place,
He lies beneath my shoe.

His tactless, disconcerting way
Of aureoling my head
Has docked him of his little day,
And turned his form's organic play
To matter thinly spread.

By what compulsion he was driven
To court contention thus,
And why that vibrant orbit given,
May possibly be known to heaven,
But is not known to us.

The 'High Places'

SHALL the High Places once again be built,
The altars reared we worshipped at of old?
If we sin thus,—do with us what Thou wilt,
On our own heads be our abounding guilt,
O Thou whose wrath consumed the gods of gold!

Our eyes have looked on scenes that blasted sight,
Our ears heard all that War's rough tongue can say;
Blinded and stunned, we struggled towards the light,
And shall we now provoke return of night,
And, prayers and tears forgetting, fall away?

If we sin thus: if the spent wave of hate,
Re-form, greed-crested, and engulf again;
If Hope's high towers in dust disintegrate,
What Power shall stand between us and the fate
Of the whelmed, sin-bound Cities of the Plain?

Question & Suggestion

I ASKED of Life, when serpent eyes
Met mine with stony glare,
What made you thus materialize,
And tabernacle there?

Were you so little helped by Heaven,
When soldering cell to cell,
That, to despairing courses driven,
You borrowed help from Hell?

And in return for labour lent—
I guess not at the sum—
A room in your grim tenement
Is let to devildom?

A Dogmatic Statement

I AM, for all that pedants prate,
By crabbed Hegelians taught,
A subject, not a predicate,
A thinker, not a thought.

What Power soever schemed my course,
Some part was left for me,
For who that once has known remorse
Doubts ever will is free?

No tool of blind unfeeling Fate,
Or mechanistic Whole,
I that, created, can create
Am Person, Self and Soul.

A 'Beauty Spot'

THAT others share a scene so fair
Should be an added joy,
But some who come for treasure there
Mix with its gold alloy.

Even those who boast its beauty most,
And sing of what they see,
Will leave it the dishonoured ghost
Of what it used to be.

A coming time will count it crime,
And some will add—a sin,
To leave like snail a trail of slime,
Like snake a festering skin.

O could I pile some desert isle
With all they reckon bliss,
And to that paradise beguile
Those who are spoiling this!

The Chief Scout

HE found in boyhood an unfurrowed field,
In wistful eyes saw glint of smothered fires;
He knew what promise lay in sap congealed,
What wild excess may spring from balked desires.

He waved his wand—Sap surges on to flower,
Sealed fountains play, dulled eyes are flushed with
flame,
Long-wasting sinews wake to sudden power,
And age grows young at Baden-Powell's name.

Use & Beauty

USE and Beauty, long allies,
Fall at strife, and Beauty flies,
Seeking aid with anguished eyes.

Tiffs and tilts had been before,
Questioning which had woven more
The unsullied robe once England wore;

Which in sooth were fairer scene,
Beauty's wild-wood tangled green,
Or cultured autumn's golden sheen;

Brook-bound meadows, cattle-browsed,
Lichened eaves where swallows housed,
Or lilied fen-lodes, idly drowsed.

Use would vaunt his vine-clad cots,
Beauty her untended plots
Of wind-flowers and forget-me-nots;

Use, his hedge-rows' bloom and feather,
Beauty, wastes of upland heather,
But O their hearts beat true together!

Trivial enmities forgetting,
Each the other's cause abetting,
Use would serve as Beauty's setting.

Now, alas! they flame apart,
Not a day but sees a dart
Aimed by Use at Beauty's heart.

Battling maenads! Sound a truce,
Beauty, bind those tresses loose;
Take her to thy bosom, Use!

Gift of Song

SONG should be built of air
   With passion charged and noble meaning, yet
   That there is more than music there
Should guile us to forget.

And let that passion's play
Be as the light flashed down from sea to shore
When a wave breaks, one touch, away!
Wake that wild string no more.

Beauty ne'er shows so well
As when unknowing that she shows at all,
And the world-singers weave their spell
Scarce conscious of their call.

But few, alas! are they
That own the unerring beat of careless wing,
Yet to far zones they point the way,
Where all may soar and sing.

A Winter Hoard

SOUNDS as of padding feet
And snarling breath warn me of Winter near—
Gaunt hungering Winter—but a barred retreat
Shall balk his malice, when his glistening fangs
 appear.

There shall his rage be spent
In the tempestuous urging of his snows,
That on me fall as idly impotent
As summer breath that stirs the petals of a rose.

That bleak, storm-leaguered hold,
In outward air foreshadow of the tomb,
Gleams inly bright with memory's hoarded gold,
By thrifty manhood stored, to ransom age from
 gloom.

Time there draws back his flow,
And renders up my past without its pain;
If it so please me—gone is Winter's snow,
Spring and her flowers are here, and I am young
 again;

And at my will I hear
Each sound that ever brought my soul delight—
Voices of friends, the sea, the lapping mere,
The song of mating birds, the waterfall by night.

Should inward ear and eye
O'ercharged wax weary of their picturing play,
They shall give place to thought, and thought shall ply
Its guiling arts to charm that weariness away.

If thought itself should fail,
As o'er the mind grey films of evening form,
Hope and desire of things beyond the veil
Shall lead me to the door, and with me face the storm.

The Trial of Reason

DOWERED by Themis with her scales,
Wielding once Athene's spear,
O forlorn Reason! What avails
To plead thy god-given glories here?

Aloft an ermined upstart sits,
Charged with the unwisdom of the day;
Prosecutors are the wits
That to the new light led the way.

'Under Reason's rule' (they urge)
'Passion never met its due;
Inhibitions checked its surge,
And chafed the emancipated few.

Her besotted laws forbid,
In a crabb'd Catonian way,
All that Dionysians did,
And youth is free to do to-day.

Instinct has sufficed the brute,
Let it then suffice the man,
Since they share a common root,
And it was there ere thought began.

Reason bade us count the cost
Of force extolled and faith decried,
Ere some Rubicon be crossed,
And some Caesar deified.'

Thus and thus they witness bear
To their thought-encumbered state,
While the judge, with vacuous stare,
Ponders on a fitting fate.

As once in Jerusalem
Ignorance judged and Wisdom died,
Who can doubt he will condemn,
And Reason will be crucified?

Old Hodge

By some unstudied alchemy, on his lips
Dull leaden gossip takes a tinge of gold,
And twinkling bubbles rise as memory dips
Far down in days of old.

Frugal of utterance, pondering word and phrase,
And parting with them only under stress,
He knows the use of measure; of all he weighs
No word falls meaningless.

His wit, a once keen weapon, from its sheath
Of passive contemplation, oft is drawn;
Cool-cellared, home-brewed wisdom lies beneath
The room where wit is born.

Nature lies open to him, as she lies
To none but those who can her counsel keep;
He has foreknowledge of her changing skies,
Whether they smile or weep.

Schooled in submission, tolerant of his kind,
Unenvious of another's easier lot,
He guards each gracious memory, casts behind
All that is best forgot.

No toil-soured boor, no peevish peasant he,
Or serf of town-bred Zola's slanderous tales;
Not Zola's self stood forth more sturdily
When justice fouled her scales.

And they that round the inn's snug inglenook
Gather nightly, and in solemn conclave sit,
Draw from him knowledge never embalmed in book
But spiced by homely wit.

The Delectable Mountains

THOSE heaven-reared hills, the pale of Paradise,
Seen through the tears of Eden's exiled pair,
Were not more fair
Than yon far lines of blue to my young eyes.

My childhood's faith was—could I reach their rim
And part the clouds that ring their shadows round,
The faint far sound
Would greet mine ears of quiring seraphim;

And the pure light that, lingering on each crest,
Lays there its last warm touch so lovingly,
Would fall on me,
Charged with some blessing from the Ever-blest;

And still in dreams they keep their ancient power
To stir my soul, those reverenced hills of mine;
Still on me shine
Those lingering rays, as in far childhood's hour.

Age to Youth

OUR rule, you say, brought things to such a
pass
That you have turned from all our thoughts
and ways;
A once-green earth's a waste of withered grass,
And you would set that waste, our world, ablaze.

You would dig deep, till surer base be found
For your new faiths than where we built our own,
You would grow fairer flowers on kindlier ground
Than where the seeds of hate and war were sown.

You fling—so foul the mess the old men made—
The clothes they wore, the forms they used, away,
And face the future naked and unafraid,
Till defter looms weave sounder stuff than they.

Ours was the age of Reason, Reason led
To ruin's door, you her cold rigours spurn,
Bid genial Intuition rule instead,
And all her pedant postulates unlearn.

Too far, too fast, that tide of impulse flows,
And Reason soon shall win recovered sway;
Yet you did well to shake us from repose;
Spend, ere yourselves shall sleep, a nobler day!

The Deposed Atom

LONG did thy honoured name express
   Supreme, unchallenged littleness,
   The small that never can be less,

Emergent Matter, the primal root
From which all grosser bodies shoot,
A Lilliputian Absolute.

But now—alas for fallen state!
Men deem thee relatively great,
A pitiful penultimate,

And put electrons in thy place—
A volatile, mercurial race—
Who play weird pranks with time and space.

And what art Thou?—The encircling deep,
Where these their settled orbits keep
(Save for one disconcerting leap!).

But chafe not at their upstart sway;
There dawns the inevitable day
Of things more ultimate than they.

For Matter's being is in debate;
On tip-toe seers and savants wait
To see it die and dissipate.

And even the electric charge—
Its last faint trace—may yet be large
To something on creation's marge.

Thy fallen state will gall thee less
If all dissolves in nothingness,
Or mere ethereal strain and stress.

Wizardry

THE breath of Beauty, on thy lips
Condensed, as Music flows,
And he that there seeks honey sips
The fragrance of the rose.

Thy subtly-fused perfections thus
The senses all confound,
Till seas are solid earth to us,
Stars jewelled points of sound.

As thou art near, or thou away,
The seasons change their place;
To greet thy coming flowers of May
Will smile in Winter's face.

Thy leaving stays the lifting lids
And opening eyes of Spring,
The bursting of her buds forbids,
Forbids her birds to sing.

Nor shall this interchange of parts
Season and Sense forgo,
Till Love, grown tired of fooling hearts,
Unstrings that wizard bow.

Ghosts as Guests

THOUGH many have, shuddering, said they see,
No vision is ever vouchsafed to me,
In this mouldering home of mystery.

Some wanting subtlety of sense
Bars me from such experience,
Or lack of faith has given offence.

I never have watched a shadow flit
From chamber to chamber and followed it,
Or seen it sitting where I would sit.

On me no muffled whisperings fall
From the cobwebbed rafters of the hall;
No flickering light steals round the wall.

No fleshless finger ever shook
The shrivelling pages of my book,
Or other unhallowed liberty took;

And never a midnight creak of stair,
An arctic blast, or a charnel air,
Brought strange uplifting to my hair.

For ages life, in joy or in gloom,
Cradled, or shadowed by the tomb,
Has known the narrow Norman room,

Where murder once—or so 'tis said—
Stood with red hand beside the bed,
Where rests my placid dreaming head;

Yet no cadaverous spectre pale,
With a sickening thud, or a withering wail,
Helps me to reconstruct his tale.

'Tis a churlish ghost that will hold aloof
From a host that harbours him under his roof,
And asks for nothing but sight and proof!

Hero v. Zeitgeist

'It is absurd to whittle down the great personalities of history
into mere typical developments of the tendencies of an age
or a race, or to make the hero a mere incarnation of the
Zeitgeist.'

(Sir Charles Oman. Inaugural Address to the Historical Asso-
ciation at Oxford. Reported in *The Times* of Jan. 3, 1929.)

RISE! Heroes, rise! Relenting Clio calls;
　　Reclaim your niches, mount your pedestals;
　　The shameful word's unsaid that shook you
　　down,
And worked like winter in each laurel crown.
The changeful Muse's reconsidered laws
Promote you now from consequence to cause.
It was but yesterday she sternly said—
'Have done with homage to the "mighty dead,"
Your kings were pawns, your leaders were the led.
If some proud deed shines forth from history's
　　page,
Its author was the "Spirit of Age."
You were at most but as some mountain crest,
That caught the morning beams before the rest.'—
Now, once again, the Hero stands confessed.
Not Fate but you—the melting Muse concedes,
Have been the authentic doers of your deeds.
Full half the events her panting scribes recall
Would, but for you, have never been at all.
But, lest she lapse into her former mind,
Confirm her present faith, cast glance behind
At saviours, hunters, scourges of mankind,
Then ask, were all their influence charmed away,
What would the world have been, or be to-day?

Had Greece lacked heroes, what were Europe's lack?
Or had no Martel turned the Moslem back?
(Think of stark Omar's Alexandrian sack!)
Quenched might have been the still unsullied light
That streams from Plato and the Stagirite;
Compute the cost to every eye that sees
Of a lost Pheidias, lost Praxiteles;
And feel, for measure fails, what were to us
A songless Athens, a silenced Aeschylus!
Turn now from culture saved to empire won—
What if a second Philip's puling son
Had been the first's and ruled in Macedon?
And what of Rome? Paint, if you can, the scene
Had Carthage conquered, Scipio never been;
Had Caesar faltered at the Rubicon,
Or to some tactless heir passed empire on!
Had Constantine, contented, stayed at home,
Nor by the Bosphorus built a second Rome,
Would half the world have knelt at Peter's shrine,
And counted his successors half divine?

Turn eastward—ask: Would Asia be the same,
Had she ne'er heard dread Timour's lurid name,
Nor seen him pass, a blast of withering flame?
Has it meant nought to India's teeming hive
That Conquerors came, from Kanishka to Clive,
And conquering creeds? Mild Buddha's star has set
In Ind, but eastward burns, and undimmed yet
Flames the red desert star of Mahomet.
Had Luther quailed, no glooms from Calvin come,
Would all have been the same in Christendom?
Or, in our realm, had often-plotted death
Cut short that crowned caprice, Elizabeth?

Had Charles the first owned Charles the second's
    head,
Would he have lost it, or his land have bled?
If two Pretenders had their faith disowned,
Would two dull Georges ever have been throned?
Or had a third more wisely grasped the helm,
Would he have mourned a sword-dissevered realm?
Ask the proud West,—Had all as proudly gone
Without her Lincoln and her Washington?
And what of Frederick and Napoleon?
Did not the Revolution take its start
From Voltaire's wit, and Rousseau's burning heart?

Enough! enough! Clank not an endless chain;
The Zeitgeist goes, the Hero shall remain!
Predestined deeds henceforth are out of date,
Let us hear more of Men, and less of Fate.

The Chrysopas

THERE is a gem, the Ethiops say,
    Veils all its lustre from the day,
    But ever, at the touch of night,
Shines glorious with an inner light.

So Youth, we feared, had dimmed its fires,
In sunny days of smooth desires,
But, in Earth's darkest, guiltiest hour,
They leaped from latency to power.

Let not those fires, in gloom reborn,
Draw back their ardours with the morn;
What Youth has given may none forget,
But Youth has foes unconquered yet.

Winter Beauty

Though the gardens bloomless lie,
And the sodden fields are bare;
Though the withered sedges sigh
To every gust that ruffles by,
And, round, the dead leaves rotting lie,
Still is beauty there.
Through the hedgerows shyly peeping,
In and out the wren is creeping,
And where trailing brambles spread,
Gleams the robin's breast of red.

Though the prisoned air be dank,
By the mossed, dismantled mill,
(Long has ceased its measured clank)
Though, clogged with matted osiers rank,
The swollen river brims his bank,
There is beauty still.
O'er the marshlands mists are stealing,
Overhead the rooks are wheeling,
Ere they join in ordered flight,
From the far-flung nets of night.

Though the clouds have gloomed the sky,
Through the bleak December day,
Now the sunset hour is nigh,
All in heaven are mounting high,
Where the sun's last arrows fly,
Soon to die as they;
In a sudden glory burning,
Then to tenderer tints returning,
Shreds and streaks that melt in air;
There is beauty everywhere.

Moß Eccles Tarn

O NCE but a dream, in space and time I set
thee,
On solid earth, and there thou shalt remain,
A joy to generations that forget me,
Though to myself thou art a dream again.

Nature, for all her dread of man's intrusion,
And deep distrust of his convulsive ways,
Smiled on me then, and nursing now the illusion
All was her work, appropriates all the praise.

The wild fowl haunt thee still, as at thy making
They flocked from far to watch thy waters rise;
Still on thee moving lines of light are breaking
The mirrored calm of mellow evening skies.

Though cherished dreams float unfulfilled around
me,
All are not vain whilst thou art gleaming still,
As fair as when the first webbed wanderer found
thee,
And on thee first shone imaged heath and hill.

Birth & Worth

M AN once a brute! Well, need it cause distress?
Would he be greater had he ne'er been less,
But leaped to manhood from sheer nothing-
ness?

Why shudder at the climbing of a tree?
What if he once crawled crablike from the sea
And stormed the land? All the more hero he!

Your hopes are set upon some future rise,
You would scale heights, even heaven itself surprise,
Why view past risings, then, with troubled eyes?

Or heed their scoffs who from man's lowly birth
Draw cynic questionings of his present worth,
And in his hopes find food for ribald mirth?

'Once brute,' they cry, 'brute must man ever be,
Then let his actions suit his low degree,
And make him of that nether kingdom free;

What profits it to climb a topless hill?
Unchain the passions, ease the straining will,
Where once man wallowed, let him wallow still;

Beasts were ye born, so, beastlike live and die.'—
If this be logic, logic is a lie,
And faith in reason flat idolatry!

An Aberdeen Terrier

WE live in worlds apart, for me
Yours were a noisome hell;
So little there is good to see,
So much is bad to smell.

Since first you came, a puling pup,
Four hairless inches high,
Scarce have I seen you lifting up
That earth-enamoured eye.

The Cat's keen vision guides her flight
To some dog-baffling tree,
But scent in you ne'er cedes to sight
Its old priority.

Height counts so little with your race,
So much, nose-down, you do,
That 'Flatland's' two-dimensioned space
Had well-nigh served for you.

Yet love can link the sundered spheres,
Where each must play his part,
And even difference endears,
When found in faithful heart.

Blakeney

As in her days of power and state,
   The great church stands, uplifting high
   Her lantern—long the guiding eye
Of commerce—Surely they were great

Who so could build, and day by day,
From sheltered homes could valiantly
Go forth to meet so wild a sea
As that which booms beyond the bay.

Those days are gone. There sound no more
The capstan song, the welcoming hails,
As some stout trader, fraught with bales
From eastland marts, draws near the shore.

For not to Anglian ports to-day
Turns England with her swollen needs.
They perished, but they sowed the seeds
Of empire ere they passed away.

Not all has gone; to marsh and lea
Still the migrating myriads flock,
To preen their plumes, and ease the shock
Of their long battling o'er the sea.

Not all is lost, for Beauty flies
From hearts that keep no place for her,
And with the wild sea-lavender
Builds here a home for outraged eyes,

That late have looked where, seamed and scarred,
Lies what men reverenced once. May all
Who hear the bells of Blakeney call,
Against a like despoiling guard.

Tiresias Wanted

WHERE is Tiresias? He of all Stygian shades
Alone keeps wisdom where all wisdom
fades;
The rest are famished essence, fabricked air,
Too thin for Thought to weave her broideries there.
In their bewildered flight they left behind
All but a pale eviscerate husk of mind.
Idly they babble of things dimly seen,
With a dull ache for powers that once had been.

And such are they who, if report be true,
By devious paths send dubious tidings through—
Loose shreds of utterance, pieced with pains intense,
Till they make something some will take for sense.
Where is Tiresias? Should he rise to bait,
His talk at least would be articulate.
He in intelligible terms could tell
Of that drear world which is nor heaven nor hell;

And, could we catch him in prophetic vein,
Might something add to ease Earth's present pain.
A touch of wisdom in our plenteous lack
Might shift Hope's anchor, or plot a saner track;
But if he comes not, there are still the stars,
And only folly chafes at reason's bars.
Where is Tiresias? Oracles are dumb,
Or some might say—He is too wise to come!

Insomnia

LAST night, ah bitter thought! I should have slept,
But that a darnèd dog the moon did bay,
And, at her setting, if but cats had kept,
If cats, all amorous, had but kept away.
Alas! were angels present they had wept,
To hear the things I felt constrained to say.
Nor came there respite till Aurora swept
The dust from off the door-step of the day.
If but those cats that dog, that dog those cats had
killed,
My heart's tempestuous longing had been all fulfilled.

Yet have I loved a dog, and deemed a cat
A gracious presence by a drowsy fire,
With shuddering satisfaction seen the rat,
Nipped by my dog, incontinent expire.
Much have I seen in each to wonder at,
And something, on occasion, to admire.
To win their favour have I not fed them fat,
Yea lavished on them all their heart's desire?
Yet sooth it is that oft, upon my bed,
I doom those cats and deem that dog were better dead.

'Rivers Blent'

THE winds come down from Dunnerdale,
    To frolic round the lea,
    Where Duddon's laughing waters hail
Coy fleeting films of sea;

A sea that now is quivering sand,
    And now a rippling bay,
Where land is water, water land,
    As night alternates day.

Far off in England's midmost shire,
    By homelier mead and wold,
Past Ecton Hill and Grindon spire
    Flows shy sweet Manifold.

Though west and east, fair streams, you move,
    Each to his several sea,
You meet and mingle in my love,
    Making there one melody.

So, differing hearts, to variance driven
    By some faith-wildering wind,
Though seeking each his separate heaven,
    Meet in the Eternal Mind.

A Summary

WHEN Life, new-clad in quivering clay,
　　　Entered on her vast essay,
　　　Too frail she seemed to bear the stress
Of Nature's wild impulsiveness.
She could but lift appealing glance
To the set face of circumstance,
And by responsive change of state
Each passing power propitiate.
By forms of dread encompassed round,
Thus only could escape be found,
And the first upward step be trod
From quickened dust to demi-god.

By age-long tutoring, Life at length
Took a new measure of her strength,
And, wielding powers experience gave,
Turned her late tyrant to a slave,
Her former foes to blessings sent
For Life's advance and betterment.
But long ere Nature was subdued,
Life entered on a deadlier feud,
Where clashing forces turned to strife
Of form with form, and life with life,
Whose last and fiercest phase began
When Life encased herself in Man.

Scarce conscious first and void of shame,
Man gloried in the desperate game;
But soon he sinned with open eyes,
When Mind—the measure of his rise—
Had armed with conscious craft and skill
The regents of his infant will.

And now, though milder codes and creeds
Have urged response to loftier needs;
Though many a heaven-illumined ray
Has chased the darkness from our day;
Though grim foreshadowings of fate
Have stood like spectres at our gate;
Still burns War's fire insatiate;
And each advancing art has given
Fresh power to thwart the will of Heaven.

Safety First

'THE plume-proud wife of the Fisher-king
Shares all his glory of breast and wing,
Nor bates one jot of her state in spring,

While the Mallard's spouse must guard her nest
In drab and homely drapery dressed,
When her lordly mate shows lordliest.'

'Twas thus, from out a marish lea,
In mellow flutings came to me
The voice of one I could not see.

Drawing the tangled bents aside,
I soon the ruffled singer eyed,
And to her peevish plaint replied—

'Look up to heaven where, circling high,
The wingèd Death patrols the sky,
How chanced it that he passed you by?

But for the plumage you disdain,
Your hopes of motherhood were vain,
Measure your loss against your gain!

And further to dispel your spleen,
Know that the nest of the Fisher-queen
Lies where no colour can be seen.

Why, palaced 'neath her dome of clay,
Should royal state be shorn away,
Like splendour worn in open day?

So near lies beauty to the heart
Of Nature, she will ne'er depart,
Save when Death rears his threatening dart.'

My tutoring ceased, but whether she,
Whose mentor I made bold to be,
Took it for sense or sophistry,

Was satisfied, or unimpressed,
Is a secret locked in a feathered breast,
By others only to be guessed.

To the Sun

COULD man's opinion rule thy fate,
As it can curb a king,
What revolutions in thy state
His altering views would bring!

When the first dim, deceitful ray
Of reason met thine own,
It showed thee circling with the day
Around Earth's central throne.

But time brought seers who, piercing far
   Beyond man's infant sight,
Proclaimed thee an imperial star,
   Proud Earth thy satellite.

Detraction, silenced in that hour,
   Has reared once more its head,
And, scoffing, hints at waning power
   And light diminishèd.

Thy reckless squandering of the force
   Whereon all lives depend
Foretells for Earth a slackened course,
   For Man a frozen end.

Scarce has this dolorous message run
   Its desolating round,
When in the incriminated Sun
   New founts of power are found.

'Away with traitorous doubts and fears,'
   Men cry, 'So vast this store,
'Twill lengthen out thy tale of years
   By many a million more.'

And Science, swift to make amends,
   Proves now that, passing thee,
Light from all other systems bends,
   As vassals bend the knee.

Then flame in glory, Nature's Lord!
   Fling largesse as thou wilt,
So long shall last that radiant hoard,
   We reck not what is spilt.

The Chameleon

ANOTHER fond belief has gone!
　　Upon a glorious head
　　　I set my pet Chameleon,
To turn its green to red.

It should have been 'incarnadined,'
Like 'multitudinous seas';
Alas! it looked as though it pined
From some obscure disease.

They said it fed on ambient air—
A bright poetic lie,
For I can swear its daily fare
Is mostly midge and fly.

O why is innocence deceived,
By wisdom led astray?
Full half of what I once believed
I disbelieve to-day.

I learnt the lion dreads the cock,
And now astonished hear,
That, though their meeting brings a shock,
The shocked is Chanticleer[1].

What most I prized I must forget,
Doubt even sights I see,
They say a monkey never yet
Was troubled by a flea![2]

[1] Aristotle. Recently tested at the Jardin des Plantes.
[2] Sir A. Shipley assures us that, contrary to general belief,
monkeys are singularly free from fleas.

Man ne'er was ape—some simian shoot
That blundered into mind—
Far back in some mammalian root
Their common fount we find.

No more the tag 'Natura nil
Per saltum' savour keeps,
She wins her way and works her will
By wild convulsive leaps[1].

As knowledge grows from more to more
The day will doubtless come,
When Nature, ceasing to abhor,
Will love a vacuum!

'The weather changes with the moon,'
That faith our age derides;
So be it, they will tell us soon
She never moves the tides!

When will this undeceiving end?
Our wise have lately shown
That space will warp, and light will bend[2],
And ocean lacks ozone[3].

The simplest facts I stored in youth
Now Science takes and twists;
I lean to Pilate's view of truth
And praise the Pragmatists.

---

[1] Sir O. Lodge: 'So far from Nature not jumping, it is doubtful whether she ever does anything else.'

[2] Prof. Einstein.

[3] Prof. Fowler: 'There is practically no ozone in the lower strata of air.'

Doleful Dumps

or 'Like Cures Like'

TAKE for thy harp a tossing bough,
    And for thy lute a quavering reed,
    And thou hast melody enow
To meet a doleful spirit's need.

Not where the laverock's charmed ascent
Tells listening heaven that earth is fair,
But where the cushat makes lament,
Go, take thy brooding sorrow there.

The moaning of a winter sea
On forlorn reef or shelving drear,
Shall meeter music make for thee
Than lapping waves of Windermere.

The sob and sigh of winds that rave
O'er wastes of sand and withered pine,
Or round some lone neglected grave,
Will match those wailing notes of thine.

Dark thoughts should mate with sterner scene
Than where the laughing streamlet falls;
Go, rather, where the cloven ravine
With funeral gloom the noon-day palls.

There, mid congenial sights and sound,
Lay all thy burdened bosom bare;
Bring forth thy griefs, and spread them round,
And, on thy leaving—Leave them there!

Summer-Time in Leap-Year

(March 28, 1920)

THIS day has lost an hour;
   This year has gained a day;
   Whence this usurping, over-ruling Power,
That swells our years, as leaven works in flour,
And filches hours away?

That dares to play the accountant to the Sun;
Checks o'er his ledger, draws presumptuous pen
Through questioned items, bids him stand again,
As once he stayed his course at Gibeon?

With outraged eyes we watch an impious race
Trifling with entities long deemed sublime,
See Einstein taking liberties with Space,
And Mr Willett tampering with our Time!

On St Bees Head

TIME-WITHERED bluffs! ye are things of
   yesterday
   To yon far-lying peaks, that had their birth
When Europe in her first confusion lay,
And not an Alp had reared enchanted earth.

Yet all lay once beneath the self-same sea,
That chafes below, and to it all descend;
Rock has been sand, and sand again shall be
These cliffs, those ancient hills, ere Earth shall end.

With age-long rhythm to and fro there swings
The eternal tide of Being, all things change,
Save ordering Mind, whose vast imaginings
Build and unbuild or man or mountain range.

Birth of a Flower

A BREATH of Heaven's undying bliss
　　Came once, far-wandering, here;
　　Congealed by Earth's cold, treacherous kiss,
It fell—a frozen tear.

A passing angel pitying saw,
And by some touch of power—
Some swift o'er-rule of Nature's law—
Made of that tear a flower.

And now, its former state forgot,
Its later lapse forgiven,
It lightens, by its grace, the lot
Of other waifs of Heaven.

Hope & Hate

I DREAMED of Peace—dream fair as ever grew
From the dull roots of sleep—around me lay
Such meads as Eden or as Enna knew,
Ere Sin or Dis had been.—All dimmed away,

And I stood gazing where a pillared tomb
Rose wrapped in shimmering semblance of a shroud;
Around it clustered, seen through the sickly gloom
Of winter morn, a still, expectant crowd.

Youths were they all, and touched with heavenly grace,
While yet on each fair form there seemed to rest
A dead pain's shadow; lines on every face
Told of fierce days by storm and toil oppressed.

I knew them for the Spirits that had passed
In faith that, through their passing, earth might know
Undying peace, that after war's wild blast
Cold hates might melt in love's returning glow.

They held low converse, each to other told
How he had stolen from his rest to see
His hope's fulfilment—end of an order old,
The burial of earth's outworn enmity.

While thus they stood, the slow and massy tread
Of an advancing host was heard, and all
The wreathing mists 'gan shiver, as though in dread
Of what was mustering to that funeral.

High o'er the moving ranks a banner shone,
The host's proud ensign, but so limp it hung
In that dank air, that what was writ thereon
No man might read, as to and fro it swung.

A shrill high note leaped forth from many a fife,
To meet the hollow booming of a drum;
More charged with grim expectancy of strife
They sounded, than of joy that peace had come.

Each passing warrior's visage darkly glowed,
As from some hidden fire; in every eye
A furtive gleam of exultation showed
Some dire event or strange fulfilment nigh.

They ranged them round that sheeted sepulchre,
Eyed by the wondering shades, when straight there
    blew
A moaning gust, that made their ensign stir,
While one stood forth, and back the covering drew.

Through all that heavenly band sick horror spread;
Once more on charnelled earth they seemed to grope;
For, on that swelling banner, scrolled in red,
Was 'Hate,' and on that tomb was graven 'Hope.'

Force & Reason

WHEN Force, loud thundering on his way,
Drew rein at ruin's brink,
He muttered, frowning, 'Well-a-day!
The hour has come to think.'

So Thought, pale from her prison cell,
Where sorrow dims the light,
Plied all her arts to loose the spell,
That numbed the limbs of Right.

Knot after knot her hands untied
In Folly's tangled skein;
Door after door was opened wide,
Where Force had stormed in vain.

Then Force, with loud revilings, rose,
And flamed in Reason's face—
'Thine arts bring solace to our foes,
Back to thy skulking-place!

Thy part had been to guide our course
To surer paths of gain;
Thought should be squire to knightly Force,
A rider in his train.'

So Reason to her cell retires,
To count the dark hours o'er,
Till Earth, from all her tottering spires,
Shall toll her back once more.

The Lying Compaſs

IF joy alone were gain,
  Test of all worth, and sorrow only loss,
  Life were as homeless here as, on the main,
The wide-winged ever-wandering albatross;

A fevered baffled quest
Of what a lying compass feigns to find,
A search for peace amid the waves' unrest,
For shelter in the bosom of the wind.

But when, assured at last
No home lies there, we seek quite other shore,
Our course shines clear, and anchor soon is cast,
Where neither wind nor wave need vex us more.

A Piece of Folly

I CAME at Folly's urging here,
  And Folly's price must pay,
  To look on scenes in childhood dear,
And dear in dreams to-day.

Years had not dimmed their memory yet,
Though seven long decades lie
'Twixt that blithe hour when first we met
And the tired hours shuffling by.

Alas! I little knew how much
Of dream-land's fairy gold
Would melt or tarnish at the touch
And clash of new and old.

The part the Aesopian hound had played
I played, but did reverse;
He lost the substance, I the shade,
Each found his case the worse.

But for the folly I deplore
That sent me here to see,
A thousand beauties, now no more,
Had been alive—for me.

Still had there been a home of peace,
And happy childhood's play,
Where I could nightly win release
From the dusty cares of day.

Still, at the waving of a wand,
I could transfigured rise
And drive the cows of Fairy-land
To byres of Paradise;

Steal down the meads in misty morn
To watch the hares at play,
And listen for an elfin horn,
(For more than hares were they;)

With feigned indifference saunter by
The hollow-hearted tree,
Where once an owl (they said, but I
Knew better) glowered on me;

Read warnings of enchanted ground
In whispers of the wood,
Till creeping shadows, closing round,
Rebuked my hardihood;

Launch on the pond the embattled boat,
With brazen ordnance stored,
And o'er the webbed confusion gloat,
When inch-long cannon roared;

Astride upon the harnessed horse,
The rumbling cart behind,
Exult to feel unmeasured force
Respond to mastering mind;

Plod to the shore, a weary mile,
And massy ramparts rear,
To keep the encroaching waves awhile
Within their proper sphere;

Then, fraternising with the foe,
Explore his boisterous realm,
And wild convulsed experience know
When first his waves o'er-whelm;

Far up among the orchard leaves
A wattled fortress form,
Or, buttressed round with autumn sheaves,
Defy the thunder-storm.

Pure joys, entrancing fears—alas!
It was but yesterday
That Folly broke the magic glass,
And all was rapt away.

The sage may set the things that are
Above the things that seem,
But O that I should come from far,
To wreck my dearest dream!

When next the night-rulers bid me roam,
Where once 'twas joy to press,
What shall I see?—a shattered home
In a smoke-fouled wilderness!

The Immortals

LOVE, Power, and Wisdom stoop to pay
 Their court to human Will,
  As once, a meaner part to play,
(Or so Hellenic legends say)
 There met on Ida's hill
Their counterfeits—the Olympian Three,
Who rent two worlds with rivalry.

They bid man trample pride and greed,
Set discord 'neath his ban;
Though great their power, and great his need,
They may not force, they can but plead,
Else were he less than Man;
But once, to set the sinner free,
They met and died on Calvary.

Blackthorn & Hawthorn

TWO thorns are ours, the Spring's bold wel-
  comer one—
  Men call her black, though white her bloom
as snow—
Winter with smiling scorn she bids begone,
Mocks wild-eyed March, upbraids the laggard sun,
And lives to purple Autumn with her sloe.

The other, shrinking from endearment rude
Of winds wild-wantoning, holds her beauty back,
Till by soft showers and woodland warblers wooed,
She lays aside her coy reluctant mood,
And yields the charm her scentless sisters lack.

The Little Owl

O WHAT can ail the Nightingale,
  That she no more will sing?
  I see no more adown her dale
The flash of russet wing.
When her accustomed hour has come,
And I stand listening there,
The wandering beetle's organ-hum
Floats on a songless air.

The Little Owl is a felon fowl,
And he feareth not the day;
'Tis he has chased thy Nightingale
And all her songs away.
To woods where she was ever heard
She tells no more her tale;
A curse upon the alien bird
That hunts the Nightingale!

The Mississippi Floods

'FATHER of Waters,' not to thee alone
  And thy fierce sons, lost lands their woes
    impute;
Men raised thee to a tyrant's lofty throne,
And of their own unwisdom reap the fruit.

They, who had torn dominion from the hands
Of crowned caprice, capricious power create;
Not since towered Babel flouted Heaven's commands
Has equal folly met an equal fate.

With careless greed and unforeseeing eyes
They lay the water-harbouring forests bare,
Till trickling runlets to fierce torrents rise,
Denuding earth and baffling spade and share.

Now for unmeasured leagues the weltering plain
Cowers helpless 'neath the tyrant's swollen pride:
Unnumbered homes drift downward to the main
In fragments on his devastating tide.

Yet, as of old Virginia's stubborn son
Withstood an empire's onset, time shall be
When the Great River meets its Washington,
And tamed and bridled runs from source to sea.

Drought

SHOOT all your fiery shafts amain,
 Ye storm-clouds, gathering in the west;
 Stir thoughts of Ararat by your rain;
We count your utmost fury blest;
For long have Earth's uplifted eyes
Asked pity of unanswering skies.

Loud let your loosened thunder roll,
And far and wide your bounty fling;
A trouble lifts from every soul,
Though black your scowl as raven's wing;
Your wild, tumultuous task fulfil,
Till music wakes in every rill.

Then let your wrath benignant pass,
And withered Earth shall smile to see
Death draw his shadow from the grass,
And set the imprisoned verdure free;
While in the tempest's muttering rear
The storm-cock sounds his note of cheer.

'The Gods Themselves Cannot Recall Their Gifts'

WHAT gods have given—the poets sing,
　　Not gods themselves can take away;
　　To me it seems the very thing
That they are doing every day.

They gave me strength of lung and limb
To breast the mountain, cleave the wave;
These feats are now but memories dim
From shores that Lethe's waters lave.

They gave me—not an eagle-eye,
But something that has served to see,
Yet now I fall to wondering why
It is not what it used to be.

Thought, vision, memory suffer lack—
In short, of powers I once possessed,
The better part is taken back,
And soon the gods will take the rest.

A Garden Rose

ONCE battling in the wild, men bore thee here,
　　As they had borne some warrior to his tent;
　　Nursed thee and lavished on thee nutriment,
And fenced thee from each foe thou hadst to fear.

Indwelling power, that scarce could hold its place,
Might surfeit here, but loth to unbend the bow
And nurse a napkined talent, it bade thee grow
To more imperious beauty, statelier grace.

And shall not men, like thee beset by foes
That kept each nerve, each sinew, long astrain,
Like thee released, the loosened power retain
That turned the wilding to the garden rose?

Great shame were ours if, in an equal case,
Flowers keep their gains, men but their former
  place.

Three Anticipatory Epitaphs

(1) EINSTEIN

HERE Einstein rests, if any rest there be
  For souls obsessed by relativity;
  In life his axe shone ever at the root
Of some proud thought-encumbering Absolute.
Death holds him now, but ere his force was spent,
Space shrank her bounds, light at his bidding bent,
And gravitation fled the firmament.

Nor spared he Man; one arrow from his bow
Pierced Newton, one transfixed Galileo;
Their gold he proved with dubious ore alloyed,
And threatened Ether shuddered in her void;
With shattered axioms Nature's realm was strown,
Till Death, incensed at powers that paled his own,
Shook the Imperial Thinker from his throne.

(2) HENRY FORD

HERE lies who scaled the heavens, and found the star
Some hitch their wagons to—Ford hitched a car.
Where'er propulsion grew he probed its root,
And from each plant of promise plucked the fruit.

From Day's bright orb its measured roll he drew;
From Night's funereal car its sable hue.
Not Hades' self was spared, he stooped to steal
Its tireless motion from Ixion's wheel.
Impelling fire Elijah's chariot taught.
His tractors aped the car of Juggernaut.
On rivals passed he looked with proud disdain,
As on his bridled kings looked Tamerlane.
Outpaced at last by Death's all-conquering car,
Ford triumphs still, while 'Fords' are—what they
    are.

(3) 'MR FEEBLEMIND'

HERE lies a man, whose troubled age was spent
Pondering his past, and wondering what it meant.
His faith had been there was some part assigned
None else could fill, some goal none else could find.
But as the years went by, that faith grew dim;
The world, it seemed, had little use for him.
In fields of thought he set himself to sow,
But tares would bid defiance to his hoe.
He tapped at doors that only yield to force,
And for each failure felt a vain remorse.
Of gains and losses, at the last, he tried
To render count, but in the rendering died.
So, how his balance stood does not appear,
But Heaven has honoured drafts of souls insolvent
    here.

The Ray

Low as thy foot to-day
    Thy head ere long shall be,
    For Life is but a wandering ray,
That spends one hour with thee;
But, with it, when it journeys on,
Goes what of worth that hour has won.

From form to form shall pass
That ray, and all be thine,
Each, as on earth, distorting glass,
That blurs a thought divine;
But, imaged fair, or dimmed by shame,
None long can hold that wandering flame.

Sin bends it from its course,
And bars its upward way,
Till the keen lightnings of remorse
Around that sin shall play;
But, late or soon, that ray shall rise
To sparkle in an angel's eyes.

www.ingramcontent.com/pod-product-compliance
Ingram Content Group UK Ltd.
Pitfield, Milton Keynes, MK11 3LW, UK
UKHW020447010325
455719UK00015B/463